TO:

_____

FROM:

_____

DATE:

_____

Published in Nashville, Tennessee, by Thomas Nelson. Thomas Nelson is a registered trademark of HarperCollins Christian Publishing, Inc.

Thomas Nelson titles may be purchased in bulk for educational, business, fund-raising, or sales promotional use. For information, please e-mail SpecialMarkets@ThomasNelson.com.

Any Internet addresses, phone numbers, or company or product information printed in this book are offered as a resource and are not intended in any way to be or to imply an endorsement by Thomas Nelson, nor does Thomas Nelson vouch for the existence, content, or services of these sites, phone numbers, companies, or products beyond the life of this book.

Some content has been adapted from previously published material in *Unshakable Hope.*

ISBN 978-1-4003-1529-1

Printed in China

18 19 20 21 22   DSC   10 9 8 7 6 5 4 3 2 1

Praying the Promises

Anchor Your Life to Unshakable Hope

Max Lucado

& Andrea Lucado

Thomas Nelson

Since 1798

For Rose and Max Wesley Bishop—
proof that holding onto hope is always worth it

Contents

CONTENTS

Introduction

> *[Abraham] didn't tiptoe around God's promise asking cautiously skeptical questions. He plunged into the promise and came up strong, ready for God, sure that God would make good on what he had said.*
> —Romans 4:20–21 The Message

What is shaking your world? Possibly your future, your faith, your family, or your finances. It's a shaky world out there.

Could you use some unshakable hope?

If so, you are not alone. We live in a day of despair. Many people believe this world is as good as it gets, and let's face it. It's not that good.

But as people who believe God's promises, we have an advantage. We can determine to ponder, proclaim, and pray the promises of God. We can be like Abraham, who "didn't tiptoe around God's promise asking cautiously skeptical questions. He plunged into the promise and came up strong" (Romans 4:20 The Message). We can choose to filter life through the promises of God.

For every problem in life, God has given us a promise. When struggles threaten, we can find hope by praying those promises.

- I'm feeling fearful today. Time for me to pray Judges 6:12: "The LORD is with you . . ." I will lay claim to the nearness of God.
- The world feels out of control. Time for a dose of Romans 8:28: "All things work together for good."
- I see dark clouds on the horizon. What was it Jesus told me? Oh, now I remember: "In this world you will have trouble. But take heart! I have overcome the world" (John 16:33 NIV).

After forty years of ministry, I've discovered that nothing lifts the weary soul like the promises of God. This book contains some of my favorites. Many of them are go-to promises I've turned to throughout the years to encourage others—and to encourage myself. We desperately need them. We do not need more opinions or hunches; we need the definitive declarations of our mighty and loving God. He governs the world according to these great and precious promises.

Let's be who we were made to be: People of the Promise. Let's keep these promises handy. Pray them out loud. Fill our lungs with air and hearts with hope and declare our belief in God's goodness.

God Has Made a Covenant with You

*[God] has given us his very
great and precious promises,
so that through them you may
participate in the divine nature.*

—2 PETER 1:4 NIV

UNSHAKABLE HOPE

The heroes in the Bible came from all walks of life: rulers, servants, teachers, doctors. They were male, female, single, and married. Yet one common denominator united them: they built their lives on the promises of God. Because of God's promises, Noah believed in rain before *rain* was a word. Because of God's promises, Abraham left a good home for one he'd never seen. Because of God's promises, Joshua led two million people into enemy territory. Because of God's promises, David conked a giant, Peter rose from the ashes of regret, and Paul found a grace worth dying for.

One writer went so far as to call such saints "the heirs of promise" (Hebrews 6:17). It is as if the promise was the family fortune, and they were smart enough to attend the reading of the will. Jacob trusted God's promises. Joseph trusted God's promises. Moses trusted God's promises. Their stories were different, but the theme was the same: God's promises were polestars in their pilgrimages of faith. They had plenty of promises from which to pick.

One student of Scripture spent a year and a half attempting to tally the number of promises God made to humanity. He came up with 7,487 promises![1] God's promises are pine trees in the Rocky Mountains of Scripture: abundant, unbending, and perennial. Some of the promises are positive, the assurance of blessings. Some are negative, the guarantee of consequences. But all are binding, for not only is God a promise maker; God is a promise keeper.

PROMISES FROM GOD

By the word of the LORD the heavens were made, their starry host by the breath of his mouth. He gathers the waters of the sea into jars; he puts the deep into storehouses. Let all the earth fear the LORD; let all the people of the world revere him. For he spoke, and it came to be; he commanded, and it stood firm.

—PSALM 33:6–9 NIV

"As the rain and snow come down from heaven and stay upon the ground to water the earth, and cause the grain to grow and to produce seed for the farmer and bread for the hungry, so also is my word. I send it out, and it always produces fruit. It shall accomplish all I want it to and prosper everywhere I send it."

—ISAIAH 55:10–11 TLB

God is able to do whatever he promises.

—ROMANS 4:21 NLT

No matter how many promises God has made, they are "Yes" in Christ. And so through him the "Amen" is spoken by us to the glory of God.

—2 CORINTHIANS 1:20 NIV

PRAYING GOD'S PROMISES

Lord, you are the maker and keeper of promises. Your Word does not return void. When you say you will do something, you do it. You are able to do whatever you promise. So many years ago you made a covenant with your people, and you have been faithful to that covenant.

Sometimes it is easier to put my faith in my circumstances rather than in your promises. I want to rely on myself, my earthly possessions, and the people in my life, but these so often fail me. But your promises will never fail me!

As I read through your promises, give me a new passion for them. Show me what promises I have forgotten over the years and need to cling to again. Reveal your true character to me. Remind me of the power of your love and your grace. Strengthen my faith, and teach me to lean on your Word rather than on myself.

Thank you for keeping your promises. I'm grateful for the ultimate promise I have in your Son, Jesus. Amen.

I AM . . .

I am building my life on the
promises of God. Because his word is
unbreakable, my hope is unshakable.
I do not stand on the problems of life
or the pain in life. I stand on the great
and precious promises of God.

You Will Know God

No longer will they teach their
neighbor, or say to one another,
"Know the Lord," because they
will all know me, from the
least of them to the greatest.

—HEBREWS 8:11 NIV

UNSHAKABLE HOPE

Everything in creation gives evidence of God's existence. The intricacy of snowflakes, the roar of a thunderstorm, the precision of a honeybee, the bubbling of a cool mountain stream. These miracles and a million more give testimony to the existence of a brilliant, wise, and tireless God (Psalm 19:1–4). Everything shows evidence of a purposeful design. The facts lead to a wonderful conclusion. God is . . . and God is knowable.

He has not hidden himself. He doesn't close the door to his children. He does not resist our questions or refuse our inquiries, but rather the opposite: he promises success to all who search for him. Paul said in Romans, "Since the creation of the world His invisible attributes are clearly seen, being understood by the things that are made" (Romans 1:20).

We can know more than simple facts about our Creator; we can know his heart, his joy, his passion, his plan, and his sorrows. We can know God. Of course, we will never know him entirely. God is knowable, but he is incomprehensible (Isaiah 55:8–9). Our pursuit of him must be marked by humility. We will never know everything about God. He is to us what the Grand Canyon is to the explorer: an endless array of discovery and beauty.

But that isn't meant to discourage us. The mark of a saint is that he or she is *growing* in the knowledge of God. As saints, our highest pursuit is the pursuit of our Maker. So stand firmly upon God's promise. He will make himself known to all who seek him.

PROMISES FROM GOD

The heavens declare the glory of God; and the firmament shows His handiwork. Day unto day utters speech, and night unto night reveals knowledge.

—PSALM 19:1–2

"For My thoughts are not your thoughts, nor are your ways My ways," says the LORD. "For as the heavens are higher than the earth, so are My ways higher than your ways, and My thoughts than your thoughts."

—ISAIAH 55:8–9

"Let not the wise boast in their wisdom, nor the mighty in their strength, nor the rich in their wealth. Whoever boasts must boast in this: that he understands and knows Me."

—JEREMIAH 9:23–24 THE VOICE

What may be known about God is plain to them, because God has made it plain to them. For since the creation of the world God's invisible qualities—His eternal power and divine nature—have been clearly seen, being understood from what has been made, so that people are without excuse.

—ROMANS 1:19–20 NIV

PRAYING GOD'S PROMISES

Thank you for being a God who wants me to know you. You have not hidden yourself from me.

Father, at times I have not believed in you. I have wanted more proof, more evidence. But you promised that you have revealed yourself in creation to all of your children. When doubts come, I will cling to your promise.

Your wisdom surpasses all wisdom on this earth. Your ways are so much higher than mine. I could study you and your Word for the rest of my life and still only scratch the surface of the depths of who you are. You are at once knowable and unknowable. You've revealed yourself to me, but so much of you is a mystery and always will be.

Deepen my knowledge of you, God. I want to know you more and understand you better. Reveal yourself to me through Scripture and through your creation. Reveal yourself to me through conversations and relationships. I am so grateful for the promise of a knowable God. Amen.

I WILL . . .

I will make the knowledge of God my
highest pursuit. I will stand firmly
upon God's promise that all will know
him. And as one who seeks him, I
will trust that he will make himself
known to me through the beauty of
nature, relationships, and everything
around me. He is not hidden from me.

You Are Stamped with God's Image

"Let us make human beings in our image, make them reflecting our nature."
—Genesis 1:26 The Message

UNSHAKABLE HOPE

It's easy to feel anything but important when the corporation sees you as a number, your ex takes your energy, or old age takes your dignity. Somebody important? Hardly. When you struggle with your sense of significance, remember this promise of God: you were created by God, in God's image, for God's glory (Genesis 1:26).

God created us to be more like him than anything else he made. He never declared, "Let us make oceans in our image" or "birds in our likeness." The heavens above reflect the glory of God, but they are not made in the image of God. Yet we are.

To be clear: no one is a god except in his or her own delusion. But everyone carries some of the communicable attributes of God. Wisdom. Love. Grace. Kindness. A longing for eternity. These are just some of the attributes that set us apart from the farm animal and suggest that we bear the fingerprints of the Divine Maker. We are made in *his image* and in *his likeness*.

And the work of shaping us into his image is ongoing. As we fellowship with God, read his Word, obey his commands, and seek to understand and reflect his character, something wonderful emerges. Or, better stated, *Someone* wonderful emerges. God comes out of us. We say things God would say. We do things God would do.

You were made in his image, and you are being shaped into his likeness. When the world says you are worthless, remember this gives you infinite worth.

Promises from God

As for me, I will see Your face in righteousness; I shall be satisfied when I awake in Your likeness.
—Psalm 17:15

For You formed my inward parts; You covered me in my mother's womb. I will praise You, for I am fearfully and wonderfully made.
—Psalm 139:13–14

But whenever anyone turns to the Lord, the veil is taken away. Now the Lord is the Spirit, and where the Spirit of the Lord is, there is freedom. And we all, who with unveiled faces contemplate the Lord's glory, are being transformed into his image with ever-increasing glory, which comes from the Lord, who is the Spirit.
—2 Corinthians 3:16–18 niv

You have taken off your old self with its practices and have put on the new self, which is being renewed in knowledge in the image of its Creator.
—Colossians 3:9–10 niv

PRAYING GOD'S PROMISES

Lord, you created everything, and everything you've created is wonderful. You created me, but not only that, you created me in your image.

On the days when I feel like I am not enough or unimportant, help me remember that you cherish me because I am your child. Show me how to live as an image bearer of you. Show me how I can reflect your goodness to others and how I can walk confidently knowing that I am worthy simply because I am yours. Continue to refine me and mold me into your image until the day I see you face to face.

Thank you for loving me, for never giving up on me, and for giving me more value than anything or anyone on this earth ever could. Amen.

I AM . . .

I am worthy because God made
me in his image. He cherishes me
because I resemble him, because I
am his child. As his image bearer,
I will cling to the promise that I
am stamped with his image.

The Devil's Days Are Numbered

*The God who brings peace
will soon defeat Satan and
give you power over him.*
—ROMANS 16:20 NCV

Unshakable Hope

The Bible names a real and present foe of our faith: the devil. The Greek word for "devil" is *diabolos*, and it shares a root with the verb *diaballein*, which means "to split."[2] The devil is a splitter, a divider, a wedge driver. He divided Adam and Eve from God in the garden and would like to separate you from God as well. He wants to take unbelievers to hell and make life hell for believers.

Every conflict is a contest with Satan and his forces. For that reason "though we walk in the flesh, we do not war according to the flesh. For the weapons of our warfare are not carnal but mighty in God for pulling down strongholds" (2 Corinthians 10:3–4).

What are our weapons? Prayer, worship, and Scripture. When we pray, we engage the power of God against the devil. When we worship, we do what Satan himself did not do: we place God on the throne. When we pick up the sword of Scripture, we do what Jesus did in the wilderness. He responded to Satan by proclaiming truth (Matthew 4:1–11). And since Satan has a severe allergy to truth, he left Jesus alone.

Satan will not linger long where God is praised and prayers are offered. Satan may be vicious, but he will not be victorious. The devil is a defeated devil (Jude v. 6), so don't give him more than a passing glance. God has already won.

PROMISES FROM GOD

Our fight is not against people on earth but against the rulers and authorities and the powers of this world's darkness, against the spiritual powers of evil in the heavenly world. That is why you need to put on God's full armor. Then on the day of evil you will be able to stand strong.

—EPHESIANS 6:12–13 NCV

Having disarmed the powers and authorities, [Jesus] made a public spectacle of [the forces of evil], triumphing over them by the cross.

—COLOSSIANS 2:15 NIV

Therefore submit to God. Resist the devil and he will flee from you.

—JAMES 4:7

But I want to remind you, though you once knew this, that the Lord, having saved the people out of the land of Egypt, afterward destroyed those who did not believe. And the angels who did not keep their proper domain, but left their own abode, He has reserved in everlasting chains under darkness for the judgment of the great day.

—JUDE vv. 5–6

PRAYING GOD'S PROMISES

God, you are all-powerful. No evil can defeat you. No one can come against you. You defeated death itself. You are victorious over all. The devil has no authority next to you. With just the mention of your name, he runs in fear.

Out of my own strength, I give in to Satan's temptations every day. I wake up determined not to commit the same sins I did yesterday, yet each day, I do. Sometimes I choose the path that is most convenient instead of what is righteous. Lord, forgive me, and help me remember that I can overcome any temptation when I rely on your strength.

Keep me from evil, not just in my actions, but in my thoughts and my heart. Give me scripture with which to guard myself when temptation comes. Protect my mind. Keep me alert to false promises and false teaching.

I am so grateful that in Christ, I do not have to fear the evil one. In Christ, I can be certain that evil will not conquer me because it has already been conquered. Amen.

I WILL . . .

I will acknowledge Satan but worship God. I will trust that Christ is greater than any temptation that will come my way. I will not rely on my own strength when I come face to face with the evil one. I will guard my heart and mind with God's truth.

Troubles Come,
but So Does God

*By faith Noah, when warned
about things not yet seen, in
holy fear built an ark to save
his family. By his faith he
condemned the world and
became heir of the righteousness
that is in keeping with faith.*

—HEBREWS 11:7 NIV

UNSHAKABLE HOPE

Before sending the Flood that would cover the earth, God promised safety for Noah and his family. All of humanity at the time was wicked, "but Noah found grace in the eyes of the LORD" (Genesis 6:8). This is the first time we see the word *grace* in Scripture. We might expect *grace* to debut in David's psalm or Jesus' sermon or Paul's epistle. But it doesn't. Grace comes when the Flood does.

Noah found a God who would stoop down and help him. Indeed, "stoop" is the Hebrew meaning of the word *grace*. God stooped and entered Noah's world. Grace is the God who stoops, who descends, who condescends and reaches.

The Noah story is our story. The world is corrupt. The judgment is sure. But the salvation is certain. God has provided us a way of escape: "For all have sinned and fall short of the glory of God, and all are justified freely by his grace through the redemption that came by Christ Jesus" (Romans 3:23–24 NIV).

God promised to stoop down to Noah's level by saving him from the Flood. God then stooped down to our level in the form of Jesus to save us from our sin. We were in trouble, but he came near.

We are saved, not by a boat, but by Jesus Christ. He is our Ark. We enter into him. We trust him. His gangplank is made of Calvary's cross. The skylight is formed from an empty tomb. He seals it shut from the outside. He, and he alone, keeps us safe from the evil that floods about us. When we trust the promises of God, we enjoy the unspeakable benefit of his Son.

PROMISES FROM GOD

For by grace you have been saved through faith, and that not of yourselves; it is the gift of God.

—EPHESIANS 2:8

In [the ark] only a few people, eight in all, were saved through water, and this water symbolizes baptism that now saves you also—not the removal of dirt from the body but the pledge of a clear conscience toward God. It saves you by the resurrection of Jesus Christ.

—1 PETER 3:20–21 NIV

"For in the days before the flood, people were eating and drinking, marrying and giving in marriage, up to the day Noah entered the ark; and they knew nothing about what would happen until the flood came and took them all away. That is how it will be at the coming of the Son of Man. . . . So you also must be ready, because the Son of Man will come at an hour when you do not expect him."

—MATTHEW 24:38–39, 44 NIV

He is able, once and forever, to save those who come to God through him. He lives forever to intercede with God on their behalf.

—HEBREWS 7:25 NLT

PRAYING GOD'S PROMISES

Father, our world seems increasingly evil, and we are in need of rescuing. And like you did in the days of Noah, you have provided a vessel of escape for all of your children through Jesus. You care for your children so much that you sent your own Son to dwell among us so that we might be reconciled to you through grace.

Help me rely on your promise of grace because I have been found righteous through Jesus. When troubles come, use those troubles to increase my faith and draw me nearer to you.

Each step and breath I take is because of the grace you have given me. It is the greatest gift I will ever receive. I am in awe that when I was in trouble, you came near. Amen.

I WILL . . .

I will respond to troubles with increasing
faith. I will rely on God's promise of grace
because I have been found righteous
in his sight through Christ. I will live
freely because his grace has rescued me.

You Are Made Right by Faith

*Therefore it is of faith that it might
be according to grace, so that
the promise might be sure to all
the seed, not only to those who
are of the law, but also to those
who are of the faith of Abraham,
who is the father of us all.*

—ROMANS 4:16

Unshakable Hope

The apostle Paul loved to talk about Abraham. In his fourteen letters he made nineteen references to the patriarch. He spoke of Abraham more than he spoke of anyone except Jesus. Abraham was Paul's poster child for salvation by faith.

Abraham, remember, predated the law of Moses. Abraham was saved by God before God gave the law. As Paul said, "Abraham believed God, and it was accounted to him for righteousness" (Romans 4:3).

When was Abraham's faith credited to him as righteousness? It was before Abraham had done any work. This has huge ramifications. If Abraham was saved apart from lineage and law, then what does this say about Gentiles and law-breakers like me? I am not of the bloodline of Abraham nor have I kept the law to perfection. Does God have a place for people like me? Yes!

Those who trust in Christ are included in the blessing of Abraham. We are seen as a part of the family. Gone is the fear of falling short! Gone is the anxious quest for right behavior. Gone are the nagging questions: *Have I done enough? Am I good enough?*

God's promise to Abraham was salvation by faith. God's promise to you and me is salvation by faith. Just faith. Stand on this promise.

Promises from God

Then He brought him outside and said, "Look now toward heaven, and count the stars if you are able to number them." And He said to him, "So shall your descendants be." And he believed in the Lord, and He accounted it to him for righteousness.

—Genesis 15:5–6

Salvation comes no other way; no other name has been or will be given to us by which we can be saved, only this one.

—Acts 4:12 the message

And to one who does not work but trusts him who justifies the ungodly, his faith is reckoned as righteousness.

—Romans 4:5 rsv

If anyone else thinks he may have confidence in the flesh, I more so: circumcised the eighth day, of the stock of Israel, of the tribe of Benjamin, a Hebrew of the Hebrews; concerning the law, a Pharisee; concerning zeal, persecuting the church; concerning the righteousness which is in the law, blameless. But what things were gain to me, these I have counted loss for Christ.

—Philippians 3:4–7

Praying God's Promises

Father, sometimes I convince myself that I need to earn your salvation. I feel like I should do more, be more, and achieve more. But you simply want my faith.

Help me let go of my striving and this need to perform for you and for others. I know you want more than good deeds and religious acts—you want my belief in your promises.

You are a God of grace and love. Your well runs deep, and there is no limit to your mercy and forgiveness. You seek reconciliation with all of your children through faith in Jesus.

Thank you for canceling the debt I never could have paid and for crediting my faith as righteousness in Christ. Amen.

I WILL . . .

I will rest in the assurance of salvation.
I will stand on the promise that my
debt has been paid. I will no longer feel
as if I am falling short or not enough.
My faith has been credited to me as
righteousness through Christ Jesus.

God Will Bring
Good from Evil

*"I'll see to it that everything
works out for the best."*
—I<small>SAIAH</small> 54:17 T<small>HE</small> M<small>ESSAGE</small>

UNSHAKABLE HOPE

Joseph's story is one of abandonment. His brothers disliked his dreams and swagger and decided to throw him in a pit and feed him to the wild animals. His father, Jacob, is, tellingly, unmentioned. If Jacob ever raised a concern, we don't read about it. Potiphar's wife accused Joseph of rape, and her husband took her side over Joseph's, tossing him in prison for a crime he didn't commit.

Yet, it was through suffering that Joseph came to be God's tool of rescue to the Hebrew people. Joseph went from prison to a palace. He interpreted the dream that forecasted a famine. Pharaoh promoted him to prime minister, where Joseph successfully navigated the crisis and saved not just the Egyptians, but the family of Jacob.

Later Joseph would tell his brothers, "You intended to harm me, but God intended it for good" (Genesis 50:20 NIV).

Can he not do the same for you? Maybe you weren't thrown in jail, but you were placed in a hospital, bankruptcy court, or, then again, maybe you were thrown in jail. And you're wondering, "Does God care?"

Scripture says yes. "[Jesus] is before all things, and in him all things hold together" (Colossians 1:17 NIV). God maintains everything, and he uses everything to accomplish his will.

Only in heaven will we be able to see God's purposes. Between now and our homecoming, we can only do what Joseph did. We can trust. We can wait. We can pray. And we can believe.

Promises from God

"You intended to harm me, but God intended it for good to accomplish what is now being done, the saving of many lives. So then, don't be afraid. I will provide for you and your children." And he reassured them and spoke kindly to them.

—Genesis 50:20–21 niv

You alone are the Lord; You have made heaven, the heaven of heavens, with all their host, the earth and everything on it, the seas and all that is in them, and You preserve them all. The host of heaven worships You.

—Nehemiah 9:6

We can rejoice, too, when we run into problems and trials, for we know that they help us develop endurance.

—Romans 5:3 nlt

In Him also we have obtained an inheritance, being predestined according to the purpose of Him who works all things according to the counsel of His will, that we who first trusted in Christ should be to the praise of His glory.

—Ephesians 1:11–12

PRAYING GOD'S PROMISES

God, I believe you are sovereign over my life. You made the heavens and the earth and all that is in them. You are Alpha and Omega, the beginning and end. You are outside of time. You know everything that will happen, and you have planned it according to your purpose and will.

It is not always easy for me to trust in your sovereignty. I sometimes wonder if you care about me and what's happening in my life. Forgive me, Father, for times when I may doubt your ways and your goodness. Restore my faith in you when it is weak.

Guide me during the difficult times. Give me hope as I pray and wait. Remind me of your power and authority so that I will trust your ways, even when I can't see where the path before me is going.

I am so grateful that you are in control. Thank you for your promise to turn evil into good. May I trust in that promise today. Amen.

I WILL . . .

I will trust God in difficult seasons. I will
wait and pray and believe. I will place
my hope in this truth: God works for the
good of those who love him, who have
been called according to his purpose.

God Will Guide You

Jesus performed many other signs
in the presence of his disciples,
which are not recorded in this book.
But these are written that you may
believe that Jesus is the Messiah, the
Son of God, and that by believing
you may have life in his name.

—JOHN 20:30–31 NIV

UNSHAKABLE HOPE

U p until the miracle on Mount Sinai, God had spoken to his creation. He had spoken through divine decrees. He had spoken through direct address. He had spoken through human lips. God's words had come through a variety of ways. But the miracle on Sinai inaugurated a new era of God's written word: "When the LORD finished speaking to Moses on Mount Sinai, he gave him the two tablets of the covenant law, the tablets of stone inscribed by the finger of God" (Exodus 31:18 NIV).

I envision a lightning-like finger chiseling word after word into stone. If Moses was able to move, it was only to gulp or pray. Upon completion, the stone tablets were given to Moses to, in turn, give them to people. In doing so, God gave us this promise: he will guide us.

Of all the forms of God's communication, his written word is most widespread. What began on Sinai continued through Joshua, who recorded God's word in the Book of the Law (Joshua 24:26); Isaiah, who instructed that his prophecy be written and recorded (Isaiah 30:8); and the many writers of the New Testament.

The written word changed the way God related to his people. We were not present to hear his decrees. Many of us are not privy to personal, divine conversations. But we can have a Bible. We can read God's decrees through his written Word. We can inspect and reflect upon them personally and endlessly.

When you set your heart to be a person of the Bible, you can trust God's promise that he will show you the way you should go.

Promises from God

Assemble the people—men, women and children, and the foreigners residing in your towns—so they can listen and learn to fear the Lord your God and follow carefully all the words of this law. Their children, who do not know this law, must hear it and learn to fear the Lord your God as long as you live in the land you are crossing the Jordan to possess.

—Deuteronomy 31:12–13 niv

I will instruct you and teach you in the way you should go.
—Psalm 32:8 niv

"Then you will know the truth, and the truth will set you free."

—John 8:32 niv

All Scripture is inspired by God and profitable for teaching, for reproof, for correction, for training in righteousness; so that the man of God may be adequate, equipped for every good work.

—2 Timothy 3:16–17 nasb

PRAYING GOD'S PROMISES

God, thank you for communicating with your people. I know it is by your truth that I am set free, and I am so grateful that I have access to your truth through your Word.

You spoke creation into being. Your word is powerful. What you say is true and good and just. All Scripture has been inspired by you. You have given us your Word in written form so that we might know you and be guided by you.

Forgive me when I look for guidance outside of your Word. When I ask friends what to do before I open my Bible. When I am resistant to reading your Word because I want to guide myself rather than be guided by you.

Renew my desire and passion for reading the Bible. I want to get to know you better, and I know I can only do that by reading what you have said. May I learn something new about you and your character each time I read it. May our relationship deepen as I open your Word more and more. Amen.

I WILL . . .

I will read and heed God's Word. It will occupy the highest place in my life. I will depend on it first and foremost for guidance, for it is by knowing the truth that I am set free. I will build my life on the promises of Scripture.

You Are an Heir of God

*God's Spirit touches our spirits
and confirms who we really
are. We know who he is, and we
know who we are: Father and
children. And we know we are
going to get what's coming to us—
an unbelievable inheritance!*

—Romans 8:16–17 The Message

Unshakable Hope

Glistening in the jewel box of God's promises to you is a guarantee of your inheritance: you are an heir—an heir of God and coheir with Christ (Romans 8:17).

You aren't merely a slave, servant, or saint of God. No, you are a child of God. You have legal right to the family business and fortune of heaven. The will has been executed. The courts have been satisfied. Your spiritual account has been funded. He "has blessed [you] with every spiritual blessing in the heavenly places in Christ" (Ephesians 1:3).

Divine resources have been deposited in your heart. You have everything you need to be everything God desires. Need more patience? It's yours. Need more joy? Ask for it. Running low on wisdom? God has plenty. Put in your order.

Your Father is rich. "Yours, O Lord, is the greatness, the power, the glory, the victory, and the majesty. Everything in the heavens and on earth is yours, O Lord, and this is your kingdom. We adore you as the one who is over all things" (1 Chronicles 29:11 NLT).

You will never exhaust his resources. At no time does he wave away your prayer with "Come back tomorrow. I'm too tired, weary, depleted."

God is affluent! Wealthy in love, abundant in hope, overflowing in wisdom. In Christ, you are a new person. Live like one. It's time for you to live out your inheritance.

PROMISES FROM GOD

We are heirs—heirs of God and co-heirs with Christ.
—ROMANS 8:17 NIV

So you are no longer a slave, but God's child; and since you are his child, God has made you also an heir.
—GALATIANS 4:7 NIV

In the past God spoke to our ancestors through the prophets at many times and in various ways, but in these last days he has spoken to us by his Son, whom he appointed heir of all things, and through whom also he made the universe.
—HEBREWS 1:1–2 NIV

God is love. Whoever lives in love lives in God, and God in them. This is how love is made complete among us so that we will have confidence on the day of judgment: In this world we are like Jesus.
—1 JOHN 4:16–17 NIV

PRAYING GOD'S PROMISES

Lord, you are rich in mercy, love, wisdom, and grace. You never run out of these good gifts for your children, and you gave us the greatest gift of all: your Son, Jesus Christ. Through him, we get to spend eternity with you—a blessing we do not deserve nor one we could have ever earned.

In spite of your good and gracious gifts, my heart still longs for earthly riches. I seek wealth, success, and security, forgetting that you have already given me everything I need.

But God, you have welcomed me into your family. In Christ, I am no longer a slave to the things of this earth that will one day pass away. I am an heir of the gifts of eternity because I am yours. In you, I have an abundance of grace, wisdom, and love—the riches you provide that fulfill every empty place in my life.

Thank you for adopting me as your child. You have given me an inheritance, and I will live freely under the promise of your covering and grace. Amen.

I AM . . .

I am an heir: an heir of God and co-heir
with Christ. Because of this I will live as
a child who has the greatest inheritance
there ever was: eternal life with Christ
Jesus, my Lord. I will no longer live
as a slave, but as a free child of God.

God Is Near

The Lord is with you.
—Judges 6:12 NIV

UNSHAKABLE HOPE

God uses common people for uncommon works. Gideon, for example, was a simple sodbuster. He displayed no political ambitions, demonstrated no military interests, and yet God turned this farmer into a leader and used him to protect Israel. With only three hundred men, Gideon defeated the mighty Midianite army (Judges 7:1–25).

In this victory, Gideon learned what God wants us to learn: all we need is the presence of God. He is enough. We don't need a large army. We don't need abundant resources. His presence tilts the scales in our favor.

The same God who was with Gideon is right beside you. As David said, "Where can I go from Your Spirit? . . . If I ascend into heaven, You are there; if I make my bed in hell, behold, You are there. If I take the wings of the morning, and dwell in the uttermost parts of the sea, even there Your hand shall lead me" (Psalm 139:7–10).

The two-dollar theological term for this is *omnipresence*. *Omni* is the Latin prefix for "all." God's presence is all-encompassing. Don't apply earthly physics to him. He does not have size or spatial limitation. He is present in every point of space with his whole being.

Which means, he is with you as you face your armies. With you as you are wheeled into surgery. With you as you enter the cemetery. With you, always.

Let this promise find a permanent place in your heart. God is with you.

PROMISES FROM GOD

The LORD is my shepherd; I shall not want.... Yea, though I walk through the valley of the shadow of death, I will fear no evil; for You are with me; Your rod and Your staff, they comfort me.

—PSALM 23:1, 4

"Am I a God near at hand," says the LORD, "and not a God afar off? Can anyone hide himself in secret places, so I shall not see him?" says the LORD; "Do I not fill heaven and earth?" says the LORD.

—JEREMIAH 23:23–24

"Go therefore and make disciples of all the nations, baptizing them in the name of the Father and of the Son and of the Holy Spirit, teaching them to observe all things that I have commanded you; and lo, I am with you always, even to the end of the age."

—MATTHEW 28:19–20

"I will not leave you all alone. I will come back to you. In a little while the world will no longer see me, but you will see me. You will live because I live. On that day you will know that I am in my Father and that you are in me and that I am in you."

—JOHN 14:18–20 GW

PRAYING GOD'S PROMISES

God, you are Immanuel, God with us. You did not leave your creation to fend for itself. You have been near to us and present with us all along. Through your Son, you have saved us, and with your Spirit, you have guided us.

When I am fearful and anxious, I can forget you are here. Give me a sense of your presence. May I feel you in the quiet moments and know that you are near. When a worry arises, remind me of your presence so that I will turn to you and not fear. Help me know that it is going to be okay and that you are on my side, fighting for me.

Thank you for always being near. How grateful I am to serve a God whose tender presence I can always trust. Amen.

I WILL . . .

I will lay claim to the nearness of God. When the devil tries to tell me I'm alone, I will remember God's promise to be with me. My Father's presence guides me wherever I go. I will believe that he fights for me.

Jesus Is Your Redeemer

But the Lord *will redeem those
who serve him. No one who takes
refuge in him will be condemned.*

—Psalm 34:22 nlt

UNSHAKABLE HOPE

Kinsman-redeemer is a phrase that takes center stage in one of the Bible's great stories of romance and redemption, the book of Ruth.

A famine had driven Naomi's family from Bethlehem to Moab, where her husband and two sons died a few years later, leaving her a widow in a foreign land. She had no means to earn money, so she resolved to return to her hometown of Bethlehem. Her daughter-in-law Ruth went with her.

Boaz was everything the women were not. He was a man of means; they were women in need. He owned property; they owned nothing. When Boaz saw Ruth gleaning grain in his field, he asked about her, spoke to her with kindness, instructed her, and protected her. Eventually, he married her, saving Ruth and Naomi from ruin. He was their kinsman-redeemer.

Boaz saw Ruth; Christ sees you. Boaz was affluent. Jesus owns every square inch of the universe. Boaz spoke kindly. Jesus is tender with you. Boaz told men to leave Ruth alone. Jesus commands Satan to leave you alone. Boaz gave Ruth water and bread. Jesus loads your life with blessings. Boaz represented the women with the city leaders. Jesus represents you in heaven.

Ask your kinsman-redeemer to take you into his care. Ask him to protect you. He has promised to do so.

Redeemers offer more than one-time assistance. They rescue, yes, but they provide a home, a name, security, and a future. Your Redeemer is doing this for you.

PROMISES FROM GOD

The women said to Naomi: "Praise be to the LORD, who this day has not left you without a guardian-redeemer. May he become famous throughout Israel! He will renew your life and sustain you in your old age. For your daughter-in-law, who loves you and who is better to you than seven sons, has given him birth."

—RUTH 4:14–15 NIV

They remembered that God was their Rock, that God Most High was their Redeemer.

—PSALM 78:35 NIV

Praise be to the Lord, the God of Israel, because he has come to his people and redeemed them. He has raised up a horn of salvation for us in the house of his servant David (as he said through his holy prophets of long ago).

—LUKE 1:68–70 NIV

But when the set time had fully come, God sent his Son, born of a woman, born under the law, to redeem those under the law, that we might receive adoption to sonship.

—GALATIANS 4:4–5 NIV

PRAYING GOD'S PROMISES

Gracious Father, nobody is beyond your redemption. Because of your love and mercy, you provided a Redeemer for us in Christ, who graciously stopped us while we were on the path of sin, gave us refuge, and pointed us toward the road of redemption.

Sometimes I do not see a way out of my circumstances. I may feel stuck and bitter and doubt your provision. I don't always understand why I am on this path or how you will provide for my needs. Help me believe in the promise of Christ as my Redeemer. Help me see that no matter what my circumstances may be, my redemption is secure because of Jesus. Even if my situation never changes, I will still serve you.

God, thank you for sending my kinsman-redeemer. You sent Christ to die for me—the ultimate act of provision. I will trust you to provide for me still. In you, I have a home, a name, security, and a future. Amen.

I WILL . . .

I will turn to Christ, my kinsman-redeemer. I will depend on the promise that I have been redeemed and provided for. I will depend on Christ for every need, for he is the ultimate provider. I need nothing else but him alone. No matter what my circumstances might be, I will trust that my salvation is secure.

Giants Will Fall

*David said to the Philistine, "You come against me with sword and spear and javelin, but I come against you in the name of the L*ORD *Almighty, the God of the armies of Israel . . . All those gathered here will know that it is not by sword or spear that the L*ORD *saves; for the battle is the L*ORD*'s.*

—1 SAMUEL 17:45, 47 NIV

UNSHAKABLE HOPE

The behemoth Goliath grunted one final boast. Scrawny David loaded a single stone. Goliath raised his sword. The shepherd swung his sling. The battle was over before it began. Goliath went down. And when he did, the Philistine army ran. The Israelites, suddenly infused with courage, overtook their enemies, and a new day began for Israel.

All because David knew this: the battle was the Lord's.

David went on to fight many battles in his life. In many battles, he remembered God. In many, he forgot him. He remembered God when he saw Goliath. He forgot God when he saw Bathsheba. He remembered God and didn't kill Saul in the cave. He couldn't have been thinking about God when he opted for eight wives.

Maybe this is why we love David's story: his stained glass is cracked just like ours. David's bad days warn us to be careful. And his triumphant days remind us to be mindful. But all of them remind us to be confident because God is fighting for us.

Who is your Goliath? What giant seeks to liposuction the life out of your life? Does he come in the form of a disease? Is he wearing the garb of debt? Or defeat? One put-down after another?

"Our God will fight for us" (Nehemiah 4:20).

Lay claim to this great and powerful promise. It's not just you and Goliath. You aren't alone in your struggles. The next time you hear the bully of the valley snort and strut, you remind yourself and him, "This battle belongs to the Lord."

PROMISES FROM GOD

The LORD will fight for you; you need only to be still.
—EXODUS 14:14 NIV

The LORD your God, who goes before you, He will fight for you, according to all He did for you in Egypt before your eyes.
—DEUTERONOMY 1:30

Some trust in chariots, others in horses, but we trust the LORD our God. They are overwhelmed and defeated, but we march forward and win.
PSALM 20:7–8 NCV

In all these things we are more than conquerors through him who loved us. For I am sure that neither death nor life, nor angels nor rulers, nor things present nor things to come, nor powers, nor height nor depth, nor anything else in all creation, will be able to separate us from the love of God in Christ Jesus our Lord.
—ROMANS 8:37–39 ESV

Praying God's Promises

Lord, you are the God of armies, the defender of the weak. The battle truly belongs to you. You have defeated the evil one. No one can stand against you and your power and authority. You are fighting for me.

Forgive me when I try to fight my own battles. When I fear the loss of control or when I fear for my reputation, sometimes I try to take things into my own hands. If I try to fight for myself, I end up feeling exhausted and defeated by my own efforts. You have said you are fighting for me. Help me believe that truth even when I am so tempted to fight for myself.

Go before me this week as I face temptation. Go before me as I face anxiety, fear, and uncertainty. Protect me in every spiritual battle. Fight for me and help me surrender each battle to you.

God, I am so grateful that you are my Protector. Because of you, I don't have to fear the giants in my life. I know they will all fall at your feet, for you are the God of armies. Amen.

I WILL . . .

I will battle in the name of the Lord
Almighty. I will not try to fight on my
own. I will not fear my enemies. I will
trust in the promise that all giants fall
by the power of God, my Father. The
battle is his, and he has already won.

Your Prayers Have Power

When a believing person prays,
great things happen. Elijah was
a human being just like us. He
prayed that it would not rain,
and it did not rain on the land
for three and a half years! Then
Elijah prayed again, and the rain
came down from the sky, and
the land produced crops again.
—JAMES 5:16–18 NCV

UNSHAKABLE HOPE

I f you have taken on the name of Christ, you have clout with the most powerful being in the universe. When you speak, God listens.

Want proof? Consider the story of Elijah. He lived under the rule of the evilest of the monarchs, King Ahab (1 Kings 21:25–26).

This was a dark time in the history of Israel. The leaders were corrupt. The people worshipped Baal, a pagan god. But amidst the darkness, Elijah appeared. And with a prayer, he proved who the one true God was.

Elijah told the 450 prophets of Baal: "You ask your God to send fire; I'll ask my God to send fire. The God who answers by fire is the true God."

Though the prophets prayed all afternoon, nothing happened. Finally, Elijah asked for his turn. He prayed, "Hear me, O LORD, hear me, that this people may know that You are the LORD God" (1 Kings 18:37).

God answered immediately: "Then the fire of the LORD fell and consumed the burnt sacrifice.... [W]hen all the people saw it, they fell on their faces; and they said, 'The LORD, He is God!'" (1 Kings 18:38–39).

God delighted in hearing Elijah's prayer. God delights in hearing yours too. Why? Your prayers matter to God because you matter to God. You aren't just anybody. In Christ, you are his child.

Prayer is not the last resort; it is the first step. God delighted in and answered Elijah's prayer. God delights in and will answer yours as well.

Promises from God

"When two of you get together on anything at all on earth and make a prayer of it, my Father in heaven goes into action."

—Matthew 18:19 The Message

The eyes of the Lord are on the righteous, and His ears are open to their cry.

—Psalm 34:15

Now this is the confidence that we have in Him, that if we ask anything according to His will, He hears us.

—1 John 5:14

Therefore, since we have a great high priest who has ascended into heaven, Jesus the Son of God, let us hold firmly to the faith we profess.

—Hebrews 4:14 NIV

PRAYING GOD'S PROMISES

Lord, in Christ I have a great High Priest who has given me confidence to come before the throne to receive grace and mercy. Thank you for always listening to me.

God, it is so easy for me to go an entire day without speaking to you. I can get caught up in my own thoughts and tasks, forgetting I have a heavenly Father who is available to talk anytime, day or night. Let today be different. As concerns and questions come up, remind me to turn each of them over to you in prayer. I lift up my family to you. I lift up my work to you. I lift up my to-do list to you. Cover each worry with your peace. Prioritize my day so that it aligns with your will and not mine.

You have promised to answer when I call. So help me come before your throne in boldness and in belief, knowing you will hear me and knowing that you care for me. Amen.

I WILL . . .

Because I have a new name in Christ
Jesus, I will make prayer my priority
and passion. I will pray, knowing that my
words have power. I will believe that God
hears each one of my prayers because he
answers when a believing person prays.

God Gives Grace
to the Humble

Yes, all of you be submissive to one another, and be clothed with humility, "for God resists the proud, but gives grace to the humble."

—1 Peter 5:5

UNSHAKABLE HOPE

King Nebuchadnezzar was the uncontested ruler of the world. During his rule, greater Babylon's population reached as high as half a million people.[3] But all of this was about to end. Nebuchadnezzar thought he was in charge. For this reason, God humbled him.

Daniel warned the king of God's intentions: "Let his mind be changed from that of a man and let him be given the mind of an animal, till seven times pass by for him" (Daniel 4:16 NIV).

Nebuchadnezzar did not heed Daniel's warning.

When the mighty fall, the fall is mighty. One minute Nebuchadnezzar was at the peak of power; the next he was banished like a caged creature. And we are left with this lesson: God hates pride.

God resists the proud because the proud resist God. The heart of pride never confesses, never repents, never asks for forgiveness. Pride is the hidden reef that shipwrecks the soul.

To the degree God hates arrogance, he loves humility. Humility is happy to do what pride will not. The humble heart is quick to acknowledge the need for God, glad to confess sin, willing to kneel before heaven's mighty hand.

It took seven years, but King Nebuchadnezzar learned this lesson: "Now I, Nebuchadnezzar, praise and exalt and glorify the King of heaven. . . . [T]hose who walk in pride he is able to humble" (Daniel 4:37 NIV).

God gives grace to the humble because the humble are hungry for grace.

PROMISES FROM GOD

Though the LORD is supreme, he takes care of those who are humble, but he stays away from the proud.
—PSALM 138:6 NCV

When pride comes, then comes shame; but with the humble is wisdom.
—PROVERBS 11:2

The high and lofty one who lives in eternity, the Holy One, says this: "I live in the high and holy place with those whose spirits are contrite and humble. I restore the crushed spirit of the humble and revive the courage of those with repentant hearts."
—ISAIAH 57:15 NLT

Let nothing be done through selfish ambition or conceit, but in lowliness of mind let each esteem others better than himself. Let each of you look out not only for his own interests, but also for the interests of others.
—PHILIPPIANS 2:3–4

Humble yourselves in the sight of the Lord, and He will lift you up.
—JAMES 4:10

PRAYING GOD'S PROMISES

Holy God, you are worthy of all honor and praise. You are the King of kings, the Lord of lords. All creation worships you. All good things are from you. The greatest and richest ruler is nothing compared to who you are.

God, clothe me with the humility of Jesus. Give me a gentle spirit and a kind heart—things I cannot have when my pride gets in the way. Help me put others before myself and you above all. Give me a hunger for humility and grace.

Thank you that even when my pride wells up, you will give me another chance, and in your grace, you will humble me. Thank you for your promise to give grace to the humble. Amen.

I WILL . . .

I will pursue humility. I will not let pride be my downfall. I will put my friends' and family's needs before mine, and I will seek God's glory above all else. My humility will reflect Christ, and in that, God will be glorified.

It All Ends All Right

*In all things God works for the
good of those who love him.*
—ROMANS 8:28 NIV

Unshakable Hope

Haman had it out for the Israelites. We read about his story in the book of Esther. A few hundred years earlier, the Israelites had defeated Haman's people, the Amalekites. Haman was an Amalekite carrying a huge grudge and vendetta on his shoulders. It just so happened that Haman was promoted to a very influential position by King Xerxes of Persia. With this access to power, Haman planned to completely exterminate the Jews on Adar 13, a date somewhere around the months of February and March on our calendar.

Yet, there was another storyline developing that would eventually collide with Haman's story in a big way: King Xerxes selected a new queen, Queen Esther, who was Jewish.

What situation are you facing right now that stirs in you the same kind of fear the Jews had for Adar 13? Illness? Not enough money? Then take a tip from Esther. She used her influence as queen to talk to King Xerxes. She asked him to allow her people to defend themselves on Adar 13. He agreed. Because of this, when the day came, the Israelites were victorious and Haman was executed.

Early in his dealing with mankind, God promised to bless obedience: "If you pay attention to the commands of the Lord your God that I give you this day and carefully follow them, you will always be at the top, never at the bottom" (Deuteronomy 28:13 niv).

Esther did what was right. She took a step of faith, and God blessed her obedience. He will do the same for you. No matter what situation you find yourself in today, God will ultimately win.

PROMISES FROM GOD

This God—how perfect are his deeds! How dependable his words! He is like a shield for all who seek his protection. The LORD alone is God; God alone is our defense. He is the God who makes me strong, who makes my pathway safe.

—PSALM 18:30–32 GNT

We may throw the dice, but the LORD determines how they fall.

—PROVERBS 16:33 NLT

The sting of death is sin, and the strength of sin is the law. But thanks be to God, who gives us the victory through our Lord Jesus Christ.

—1 CORINTHIANS 15:56–58

For whatever is born of God overcomes the world. And this is the victory that has overcome the world—our faith. Who is he who overcomes the world, but he who believes that Jesus is the Son of God?

—1 JOHN 5:4–5

PRAYING GOD'S PROMISES

Almighty God, you have promised to honor obedience. Help me walk steadfastly in your Word and in your promise. Remind me of your power. Give me the courage to take steps of faith, remembering that everything will end all right.

Thank you that even if my circumstances may cause me to fear, I have the final victory in Christ. I only have to do what is right and place my trust in you. You are my hope. You are my victory.

God, you will accomplish what you set out to accomplish. You are always working for the good of those who love you. I praise you for these promises. Amen.

I WILL . . .

I will do what is right and trust God for the outcome. I will not try to manipulate or control my situation. I will let God do his mighty work, and I will serve him no matter what. He has said all will be right, and it will.

The Best Is Yet to Be

*"The glory of this latter temple
shall be greater than the former,"
says the LORD of hosts. "And in
this place I will give peace,"
says the LORD of hosts.*

—HAGGAI 2:9

UNSHAKABLE HOPE

You've probably experienced a season of God-ordained struggle, a time when there was a chill in the corner office, a dent in the savings account, a downturn. Often these days exist for a purpose: to turn our hearts back to God. Sometimes it takes a tragedy for us to hit our knees.

This is what the Israelites of Haggai's day needed. Charged by God to rebuild the temple, they had abandoned the task, distracted by worldly things. God's big thing became their small thing.

The prophet Haggai was sent to remind them of their work: "Go up into the mountains and bring down the timber and build my house" (Haggai 1:8 NIV). And he was sent to convey a promise: "'The glory of this present house will be greater than the glory of the former house,' says the LORD Almighty" (Haggai 2:9 NIV).

When nothing quenches your deepest thirsts, when droughts turn your fields into deserts and retirements into pocket change, what can you do? Evaluate your priorities: *Is God's big thing my big thing?*

The Lord stirred up the leadership of his people, and they got to work on his temple. He blessed their renewed spirit. "I am with you" (Haggai 1:13; 2:4 NIV), he twice assured them.

He is with you too. It's not too late to start again. The glory of the latter temple will be greater than the former. Or, in your case, the glory of the latter career, the latter years, will be greater than the former. Turn your heart back to him.

In God's plan, the future is always brighter and tomorrow always has the potential to outshine today.

PROMISES FROM GOD

Blessed is the man who walks not in the counsel of the ungodly, nor stands in the path of sinners, nor sits in the seat of the scornful; but his delight is in the law of the LORD, and in His law he meditates day and night. He shall be like a tree planted by the rivers of water, that brings forth its fruit in its season.

—PSALM 1:1–3

"For where your treasure is, there will your heart be also."
—LUKE 12:34 ESV

In him the whole building is joined together and rises to become a holy temple in the Lord. And in him you too are being built together to become a dwelling in which God lives by his Spirit.

—EPHESIANS 2:21–22 NIV

"Nevertheless I have this against you, that you have left your first love. Remember therefore from where you have fallen; repent and do the first works."

—REVELATION 2:4–5

PRAYING GOD'S PROMISES

Lord, you dwelt in the Holy of Holies to be a presence among your people, the Israelites. Now, you dwell in our hearts. You are always with us.

It's easy for me to get distracted by my own desires and temptations. But my efforts are always fruitless when they are apart from you and your will. Forgive me for the times when I misplace my priorities.

Give me a renewed passion for my calling, for my first love—you and your church. Reorder my priorities so that you are always first. Give me hope for tomorrow, and help me believe that the best really is yet to come when I am working alongside you.

Thank you for choosing to dwell among us, first in your temple and now, through Christ, in my heart. I praise you because it is never too late for me to start again. Amen.

I WILL . . .

I will make God's work my work. I will
keep my focus on him and his church.
I will make his will my priority. I will
do what he has called me to do. When
I don't, I will repent and, once again,
make his big thing my big thing.

God Works Through You

Therefore, my dear friends, as you
have always obeyed—not only
in my presence, but now much
more in my absence—continue to
work out your salvation with fear
and trembling, for it is God who
works in you to will and to act in
order to fulfill his good purpose.

—PHILIPPIANS 2:12–13 NIV

UNSHAKABLE HOPE

Embedded in Scripture is this astounding truth: "It is God who works in you to will and to act in order to fulfill his good purpose" (Philippians 2:13 NIV).

God offers you the same gift he gave Mary, mother of Jesus—the indwelling Christ. Christ grew in her until the miracle of gestation became the moment of delivery. Likewise, Christ will grow in you until he comes out in your speech, in your actions, in your decisions.

God promised in the Old Testament, "I will give you a new heart and put a new spirit within you; I will take the heart of stone out of your flesh and give you a heart of flesh" (Ezekiel 36:26). Who does the work in this passage? Who removes the heart of stone for a heart of flesh? God.

We do not work; we trust the finished work of Christ. Why then does Paul say, "Work out your own salvation with fear and trembling" (Philippians 2:12)? The answer is found in a simple clarification. Paul urged us to *work out* our salvation, not *work for* our salvation.

Like a growing child, we learn to walk . . . with God. We learn to talk . . . with God. We nourish ourselves on his bread and trust in his Word. Temper tantrums diminish. Prayer time increases. We seek our will less and God's will more. We cooperate with God's work, and he changes us from the inside out.

We work and struggle, but we rely on Christ's great strength. And, in time, the most wonderful thing occurs . . . we become vessels for the greatest gift of all—Jesus Christ.

PROMISES FROM GOD

"I will give you a new heart and put a new spirit within you; I will take the heart of stone out of your flesh and give you a heart of flesh. I will put My Spirit within you and cause you to walk in My statutes, and you will keep My judgments and do them. Then you shall dwell in the land that I gave to your fathers; you shall be My people, and I will be your God."

—EZEKIEL 36:26–28

To them God willed to make known what are the riches of the glory of this mystery among the Gentiles: which is Christ in you, the hope of glory.

—COLOSSIANS 1:27

To this end I also labor, striving according to His working which works in me mightily.

—COLOSSIANS 1:29

Now he who keeps His commandments abides in Him, and He in him.

—1 JOHN 3:24

PRAYING GOD'S PROMISES

Heavenly Father, I know you are at work in me. I can see the changes you've made to my heart and mind. Continue working on me and transforming me until my will and desires are aligned with yours. As you change me, allow others to see you through me.

At times I have taken advantage of your grace and not worked out my salvation. Other times I go to the opposite extreme, working too hard, working for my salvation instead of out of it. Help me find a balance where I can cooperate with your work while relying on Christ's great strength.

Dear God, only you can remove my heart of stone and give me a heart of flesh. Your Spirit can change me from the inside out. No person is too tough for you; no past is too dark. Your love enters in and transforms even the hardest of hearts.

Thank you for caring about the state of my heart. Please continue to work in me as I work out my salvation in you. Amen.

I WILL . . .

I welcome and cooperate with the inner
work of God. I will not be legalistic
and try to work for my salvation. I
will lean on Christ's great strength
and cooperate with the work of God.

God Gets You

For our high priest is able to understand our weaknesses. He was tempted in every way that we are, but he did not sin. Let us, then, feel very sure that we can come before God's throne where there is grace. There we can receive mercy and grace to help us when we need it.

—HEBREWS 4:15–16 NCV

UNSHAKABLE HOPE

We have all stumbled. In morality, honesty, integrity. We have done our best, but our finest efforts have left us flat on our backs. The distance between where we are and where we want to be is impassable. What do we do? I suggest we turn to one of the sweetest of promises: "For our high priest [Jesus] is able to understand our weaknesses. . . . Let us, then, feel very sure that we can come before God's throne where there is grace" (Hebrews 4:15–16 NCV).

God became flesh in the form of Jesus Christ. He was miraculously conceived, yet naturally delivered. He was born, yet born of a virgin.

Why does this matter? Had Jesus simply descended to earth in the form of a mighty being, we would respect him but never would draw near to him. After all, how could God understand what it means to be human? Had Jesus been biologically conceived with two earthly parents, we would draw near to him, but would we want to worship him? After all, he would be no different from you and me.

But if Jesus was both—God and man at the same time—then we have the best of both worlds. Neither his humanity nor deity compromised. He was fully human. He was fully divine. Because of the first, we draw near. Because of the latter, we worship.

Since we have a high priest who understands us, we find mercy and grace when we need it. We are not left to languish. Our God gets us.

Promises from God

For unto us a Child is born, unto us a Son is given; and the government will be upon His shoulder. And His name will be called Wonderful, Counselor, Mighty God, Everlasting Father, Prince of Peace.

—Isaiah 9:6

Jesus increased in wisdom and stature, and in favor with God and man.

—Luke 2:52

And the Word became flesh and dwelt among us, and we beheld His glory, the glory as of the only begotten of the Father, full of grace and truth.

—John 1:14

God made him who had no sin to be sin for us, so that in him we might become the righteousness of God.

—2 Corinthians 5:21 niv

For there is one God and one Mediator between God and men, the Man Christ Jesus.

—1 Timothy 2:5

PRAYING GOD'S PROMISES

Heavenly Father, you are a God of mercy and grace. You sent your Son to dwell among us so that you could draw near to us. You are a God who is with your people. There is nothing beyond your comprehension nor beyond your mercy.

Thank you for sending us your Son. Without him, I would be lost and without hope. But with him, I have every hope in the world.

God, each day I do my best to be good. Not to fail. To be patient. To live above reproach. But each day, I stumble and mess up. Help me turn to you in those moments of failure. Remind me that you understand what I am going through because Christ understands, and he is my high priest. He is the reason I can come to your throne and receive grace and mercy.

I will draw near to you because you hear me and you understand me. Amen.

I WILL . . .

I believe that Jesus was both fully
man and fully God. Because I believe
this, I will come to Jesus as my high
priest, the one who is able and willing
to help me. I will find comfort in
Jesus, who fully understands every
desire, pain, and need that I have.

Jesus Offers Living Water

"Whoever drinks of this water will thirst again, but whoever drinks of the water that I shall give him will never thirst. But the water that I shall give him will become in him a fountain of water springing up into everlasting life."

—John 4:13–14

Unshakable Hope

The Samaritan woman stopped and looked at him. The man was obviously Jewish. What was he doing here in a Samaritan city, at her well? Jews had no dealings with Samaritans at the time.

As a Samaritan, she knew the sting of racism. As a woman, she had bumped her head on the ceiling of sexism. She'd been married to five men. She knew the sound of slamming doors.

Still, he spoke to her. "The water I give will become a spring of water gushing up inside that person, giving eternal life" (John 4:14 NCV). Jesus offered this woman not a singular drink of water but a perpetual artesian well that would quench the soul.

Some of the most incredible invitations are found in the pages of the Bible. You can't read about God without finding him issuing invitations. He invited Eve to marry Adam, animals to enter the ark, David to be king, Mary to birth his Son, the disciples to fish for men, the adulterous woman to start over, and Thomas to touch Jesus' wounds.

God is a God who invites. God is a God who quenches people's thirst. But his invitation is not just for a meal or a cup of water. It is for life. An invitation to come into his kingdom and take up residence in a tearless, graveless, painless world.

Who can come? As the story of the Samaritan woman at the well reveals, whoever wishes to do so. The invitation is a promise, at once universal and personal.

PROMISES FROM GOD

With joy you will draw water from the wells of salvation.
—ISAIAH 12:3 NIV

O LORD, the hope of Israel, all who forsake You shall be ashamed. "Those who depart from Me shall be written in the earth, because they have forsaken the LORD, the fountain of living waters."
—JEREMIAH 17:13

"If anyone thirsts, let him come to Me and drink. He who believes in Me, as the Scripture has said, out of his heart will flow rivers of living water."
—JOHN 7:37–38

For you are all sons of God through faith in Christ Jesus. For as many of you as were baptized into Christ have put on Christ. There is neither Jew nor Greek, there is neither slave nor free, there is neither male nor female; for you are all one in Christ Jesus.
—GALATIANS 3:26–28

PRAYING GOD'S PROMISES

God, I can empathize with the Samaritan woman. At times I have felt like an outcast, as though nobody cares about me. I have wondered what I am worth.

But Father, from your Son, Jesus, comes living water. True satisfaction. True belonging. You quench my thirst for love and acceptance. You tell me that you are enough for me. All my desires are met in you.

Give me living water today. May your grace and mercy wash over me. Fill the holes that are in my heart with your love. When I thirst, may it be for you. When I hunger, may it be for you.

Thank you for including me in your promises. I know I am not worthy, but Christ is. When you look at me, you see him. Thank you for the promise of living water. With it, I will never be thirsty again. Amen.

I WILL . . .

I will drink from the living water of Christ. I will look only to him to quench my thirst. I will say yes to his invitation, knowing that because of his death and resurrection, I am fully worthy of the call. I know that as an adopted child of God, I never have to be thirsty again.

You Are Part of God's Kingdom

"But seek first the kingdom of God and His righteousness, and all these things shall be added to you."
—Matthew 6:33

UNSHAKABLE HOPE

The time is fulfilled, and the kingdom of God is at hand. Repent, and believe in the gospel" (Mark 1:15). With these words, Jesus not only began his ministry, but he introduced his favorite subject: the kingdom of God. The term *kingdom of God* and its Jewish equivalent *kingdom of heaven* occur some sixty times in the first three gospels.

In the teachings of our society, the same cannot be said. We don't like to talk about kings and kingdoms. We find the notion of absolute rule repulsive and medieval. Yet, this is the consistent teaching of Scripture. God is King. Did we not see the royalty of God in the Old Testament? Story after story of God creating the earth, flooding the earth, exiling his people, rescuing his people. The entire creation, both humans and nature, answers to him.

And this truth is the greatest of the kingdom secrets: the King is our Father. Remember how Jesus taught us to pray? "Our Father in heaven, hallowed be Your name. Your kingdom come" (Matthew 6:9–10).

If our Father is the King, everything changes. He listens when we call. He cares when we fall. He includes us at his table. Our King loves us, but his kingdom is not about us. It's about God.

God is creating an everlasting commonwealth, and he invites us to be a part of it. There is only one condition: the kingdom has one King. You and I are welcome to enter the throne room, but we have to surrender our crowns at the door.

PROMISES FROM GOD

Yours, O LORD, is the greatness, the power and the glory,
the victory and the majesty; for all that is in heaven and
in earth is Yours; Yours is the kingdom, O LORD, and You
are exalted as head over all.

—1 CHRONICLES 29:11

"Again, the kingdom of heaven is like treasure hidden
in a field, which a man found and hid; and for joy over
it he goes and sells all that he has and buys that field.
Again, the kingdom of heaven is like a merchant seeking
beautiful pearls, who, when he had found one pearl of
great price, went and sold all that he had and bought it."

—MATTHEW 13:44–46

Now when He was asked by the Pharisees when the kingdom of God would come, He answered them and said,
"The kingdom of God does not come with observation;
nor will they say, 'See here!' or 'See there!' For indeed, the
kingdom of God is within you."

—LUKE 17:20–21

And He has on His robe and on His thigh a name written:
KING OF KINGS AND LORD OF LORDS.

—REVELATION 19:16

Praying God's Promises

My Father in heaven, your name truly is holy. Your works are mighty. You sit on your throne. You know all and see all. Yours is the greatness and the power and the glory. Yet your kingdom is less about boundaries and castles and more about changing hearts and minds.

God, I confess that at times I want my will to be done more than I want your will to be done. I want to rule my own kingdom more than I want to be ruled by you. I want to be in charge. I want the glory. Father, forgive me.

I know the kingdom belongs to you and you alone. You are the one seated on the throne with Jesus beside you, not me. Help me remember that you are worthy of all authority. Teach me how to be a servant in your kingdom rather than someone who wants to run the kingdom.

Thank you for being a good King. Amen.

I WILL . . .

I will seek first God's kingdom. I will
worship God as the King of my life. I
will worship Jesus as my Lord. I will
live today with God's eternal kingdom
in mind. I am made for more than this
earthly life, but while I am here, I will
work to bring God's kingdom to earth.

Christ Is Praying for You

Jesus . . . is at the right hand of
God and is also interceding for us.
—ROMANS 8:34 NIV

Unshakable Hope

Lingering among the unspoken expectations of the Christian heart is this: *Now that I belong to God, I get a pass on the tribulations of life.*

To follow Jesus is to live a storm-free life, right?

That expectation crashes quickly on the rocks of reality. The truth of the matter is this: life comes with storms. Jesus assured us, "In this world you will have trouble" (John 16:33 NIV). Storms will come to you as they did to the disciples on the Sea of Galilee. They boarded their boat without Jesus and then found themselves "tossed by the waves" and a considerable distance from shore (Matthew 14:24). Like them, you may be asking, *Where in the world is Jesus?*

The answer might be as surprising for you as it was for the disciples: praying.

When the disciples came upon the storm, Jesus had gone "up on a mountainside by himself to pray" (Matthew 14:23 NIV). There is no indication that he did anything else. He prayed all night.

Ponder this promise: Jesus, in the midst of your storm, is interceding for you. The King of the universe is speaking on your behalf. And when he speaks, all of heaven listens.

Unshakable hope is the firstborn offspring of this promise. We'd prefer to have every question answered, but Jesus has, instead, chosen to tell us this much: "I will pray you through the storm."

Are the prayers of Jesus answered? Of course.

Will you make it through this storm? I think you know the answer.

PROMISES FROM GOD

Because He poured out His soul unto death, and He was numbered with the transgressors, and He bore the sin of many, and made intercession for the transgressors.

—ISAIAH 53:12

"But I have prayed for you that your faith should not fail."

—LUKE 22:32

"These things I have spoken to you, that in Me you may have peace. In the world you will have tribulation; but be of good cheer, I have overcome the world."

—JOHN 16:33

Therefore he is able to save completely those who come to God through him, because he always lives to intercede for them.

—HEBREWS 7:25 NIV

My dear children, I write this to you so that you will not sin. But if anybody does sin, we have an advocate with the Father—Jesus Christ, the Righteous One.

—1 JOHN 2:1 NIV

PRAYING GOD'S PROMISES

Lord, in the midst of my storms, I may doubt Jesus' presence. I may wonder if he is there and if he cares. Don't let me lose hope or lose heart. Deepen my belief in you, even during the storms. Don't allow doubt to take over. Help me release control of my circumstances and surrender them to you. Jesus is interceding on my behalf, and I am so comforted by this truth.

God, there is no storm you can't calm. There is no trial that is too big for you. No obstacle you cannot overcome. No hindrance that surprises you. You see all and know all. You are all-powerful, even over the mightiest of storms.

Father, thank you for sending Christ to calm the storm. Without him, I would be lost. I would have no hope in the midst of trials. But because of him, I know that I have an eternal intercessor. I know that my name is spoken in your throne room. I am so grateful to be known by you. Amen.

I WILL . . .

I will worship Jesus in the storm. I will
believe that he is interceding on my
behalf. I will take heart because Jesus is
speaking up for me. He is with me always.
I will live in the fullness of that promise.

Your Sins Are Forgiven

There is now no condemnation
for those who are in Christ Jesus.
—ROMANS 8:1 NIV

UNSHAKABLE HOPE

The algebra of heaven reads something like this: heaven is a perfect place for perfect people, which leaves us in a perfect mess. According to heaven's debt clock, we owe more than we could ever repay.

Our debt is enough to sink us, but God loves us too much to leave us. So he found a way to save us: "God sacrificed Jesus on the altar of the world to clear that world of sin" (Romans 3:25 THE MESSAGE).

God never compromised his standard of perfection. Yet he also gratified the longing of love. He was too just to overlook our sin, yet too loving to dismiss us, so he placed our sin on his Son and punished it there. "God put the wrong on him who never did anything wrong, so we could be put right with God" (2 Corinthians 5:21 THE MESSAGE).

What does this mean for us and our debt?

Each time you sin, Jesus stands before the tribunal of heaven and points to the blood-streaked cross. "I've already made provision. I've paid that debt. I've taken away the sins of the world."

Guilt simmers like a toxin in far too many souls, but you don't need to let it have a place in yours. Internalize this promise: "There is now no condemnation for those who are in Christ Jesus" (Romans 8:1 NIV).

Not "limited condemnation," "appropriate condemnation," or "calculated condemnation." That is what people give people. God gives his children *no condemnation.*

PROMISES FROM GOD

For all have sinned and fall short of the glory of God, being justified freely by His grace through the redemption that is in Christ Jesus, whom God set forth as a propitiation by His blood, through faith, to demonstrate His righteousness, because in His forbearance God had passed over the sins that were previously committed.

—ROMANS 3:23–25

For we know that our old self was crucified with him so that the body ruled by sin might be done away with, that we should no longer be slaves to sin—because anyone who has died has been set free from sin.

—ROMANS 6:6–7 NIV

For He made Him who knew no sin to be sin for us, that we might become the righteousness of God in Him.

—2 CORINTHIANS 5:21

[Jesus] personally carried our sins in his body on the cross so that we can be dead to sin and live for what is right. By his wounds you are healed.

—1 PETER 2:24 NLT

Praying God's Promises

Father, you are perfect in your ways, in your love, and in your mercy. You do not fail or fall short or sin. You are holy beyond my understanding. You sent your Son, Jesus, into this world so that I would be made holy by him and, therefore, worthy of your presence. It is only by his wounds that I am healed.

You promised that there is no condemnation for those who are in Christ, but in my heart, it's not always easy for me believe it. I may try to make myself right by doing good deeds. But I never seem to be able to do enough.

God, teach me how to live free from condemnation. Teach me how to trust and believe in this promise: in Christ, I am no longer a slave to sin. Free me from guilt and shame.

Thank you for taking care of my debt. You've ridden me of the chains of sin that had taken me captive. I now live free of condemnation, fear, and guilt. Amen.

I WILL . . .

I will find forgiveness in the finished
work of Christ. I will stand on the
promise that there is no condemnation
for those who are in Christ Jesus.
I will not let guilt weigh me down.
My debt has been paid in full. I
will live and walk in freedom.

Death Is Temporary

*Death has been swallowed
up in victory.*
—1 Corinthians 15:54 NIV

Unshakable Hope

B arring the return of Christ, you will have one final moment . . . a last gasp, a final pulse. Your lungs will empty, and your blood will still. What will you be after you die? Answers vary, but Christianity posits a startling idea: "Death has been swallowed up in victory" (1 Corinthians 15:54 NIV).

The cemetery is less a place of loss and more a place of gain. The dead in Christ are to be mourned, for sure. But they are also to be envied. Funeral dirges are understandable, but a trumpet blast would be equally appropriate.

People of the Promise hold on to the unshakable hope that hinges on the resurrection of Christ. The Christian hope depends entirely upon the assumption that Jesus Christ died a physical death, vacated an actual grave, and ascended into heaven where he, at this moment, reigns as head of the church.

The resurrection changed everything. And it proves this promise of God: he will reclaim his creation. He is a God of restoration, not destruction. He is a God of *re*newal, *re*demption, *re*generation, *re*surrection. God loves to *re*do and *re*store.

Let this hope for tomorrow bring strength to today. Your finest moment will be your final moment! Everyone else may say otherwise, that death is to be avoided, postponed, and ignored. But they do not have what you have. You have a promise from the living God. Your death will be swallowed up in victory! Jesus Christ rose from the dead, not just to show you his power, but to reveal your path. He will lead you through the valley of death.

PROMISES FROM GOD

Restore to me the joy of Your salvation, and uphold me by Your generous Spirit.

—PSALM 51:12

The angel said to the women, "Do not be afraid, for I know that you are looking for Jesus, who was crucified. He is not here; he has risen, just as he said. Come and see the place where he lay."

—MATTHEW 28:5–6 NIV

So we do not give up. Our physical body is becoming older and weaker, but our spirit inside us is made new every day. We have small troubles for a while now, but they are helping us gain an eternal glory that is much greater than the troubles. We set our eyes not on what we see but on what we cannot see. What we see will last only a short time, but what we cannot see will last forever.

—2 CORINTHIANS 4:16–18 NCV

In keeping with his promise we are looking forward to a new heaven and a new earth, where righteousness dwells.

—2 PETER 3:13 NIV

Praying God's Promises

Lord, thank you for the promise of a temporary tomb. Your power has no limits. You have conquered death. You have promised to make all things new. You are the God of restoration and redemption and regeneration. You are the God of resurrection.

In my day-to-day life it can be difficult for me to maintain an eternal perspective. Sometimes I may get bogged down in the worries of today and forget that the best is yet to come.

Restore in me the joy of my salvation, God. Renew my mind and my heart so that I will have an eternal perspective of all the worries of my day. They are nothing compared to spending eternity with you. And because of your promise of resurrection, I do not have to fear death. I will live in faith, knowing that in Jesus, death has been swallowed up in victory. Amen.

I WILL . . .

I will entrust my death to the Lord of life. I will live with eternity in mind, knowing the best is yet to come. I will not fear death, but instead, I will believe the promise that death has been swallowed up in victory.

Joy Is Coming Soon

Weeping may last through the night,
but joy comes with the morning.
—PSALM 30:5 NLT

UNSHAKABLE HOPE

Does God have a word for the dark nights of the soul? He does. The promise begins with this phrase: "Weeping may last through the night" (Psalm 30:5 NLT).

Of course, you knew that much. You didn't need to read the verse to know its truth. Weeping can last through the night. Just ask the widow in the cemetery or the mother in the emergency room. The man who lost his job can tell you. Weeping may last through the night, and the next night, and the next.

This is not new news to you.

But this may be: "Joy comes with the morning" (Psalm 30:5 NLT). Despair will not rule the day. Sorrow will not last forever. Night may delay the dawn, but it cannot defeat it. Morning comes. Not as quickly as we want. Not as dramatically as we desire. But morning comes, and with it comes joy.

Do you need this promise? Have you wept a river? Have you forsaken hope?

Joy will come. Joy comes because Jesus comes. And Jesus came because God loves you.

The greatest news in the world is not that God made the world but that God loves the world. He loves you. You did not earn this love. And his love for you will not fade if you lose your way. His love for you will not diminish if your discipline does.

You have never lived one unloved day.

God loves you, and because he does, you can be assured joy will come.

PROMISES FROM GOD

The LORD is merciful and gracious, slow to anger, and abounding in mercy. . . . For as the heavens are high above the earth, so great is His mercy toward those who fear Him.

—PSALM 103:8, 11

And the ransomed of the LORD shall return, and come to Zion with singing, with everlasting joy on their heads. They shall obtain joy and gladness, and sorrow and sighing shall flee away.

—ISAIAH 35:10

"A woman, when she is in labor, has sorrow because her hour has come; but as soon as she has given birth to the child, she no longer remembers the anguish, for joy that a human being has been born into the world. Therefore you now have sorrow; but I will see you again and your heart will rejoice, and your joy no one will take from you."

—JOHN 16:21–22

Though now you do not see Him, yet believing, you rejoice with joy inexpressible and full of glory, receiving the end of your faith—the salvation of your souls.

—1 PETER 1:8–9

PRAYING GOD'S PROMISES

Father, I confess that at times I may start to lose hope. In my dark nights of the soul, it's easy to loosen my grip on your promise that joy comes in the morning.

May those nights of weeping pass quickly, Lord. May those storms pass. Bring me joy as soon as tomorrow. Be with me in my suffering and comfort me. Instill hope deep in my soul so that I can rest, even when times are difficult.

God, you are my source of joy. You are present in the night and offer hope in the morning. You do not abandon me during my times of grieving and pain. You are with me in the difficult times, holding and comforting me until the darkness passes.

Thank you for the wonderful promise that even though the sorrow will last for the night, morning is coming. Because of Jesus, I can have joy in my darkest hour. Amen.

I WILL . . .

I will seek God even when I am sad. I
will cling to the promise that joy will
come in the morning. I will believe that
God is with me in my suffering and
that he longs to restore my joy in him.

The Holy Spirit Empowers You

"But you will receive power when the Holy Spirit comes on you; and you will be my witnesses in Jerusalem, and in all Judea and Samaria, and to the ends of the earth."

—ACTS 1:8 NIV

UNSHAKABLE HOPE

Ask a believer to answer the question "Who is God the Father?" He has a reply. Or "Describe God the Son." She will not hesitate. But if you want to see believers hem, haw, and search for words, ask, "Who is the Holy Spirit?"

Many believers settle for a two-thirds God. They rely on the Father and the Son but overlook the Holy Spirit.

The Bible makes more than a hundred references to the Holy Spirit. Jesus said more about the Holy Spirit than he did about the church or marriage. In fact, on the eve of his death, as he prepared his followers to face the future without him, he made this great and precious promise: "You will receive power when the Holy Spirit comes on you" (Acts 1:8 NIV).

The Holy Spirit is central to the life of the Christian. Everything that happens from the book of Acts to the end of the book of Revelation is a result of the work of the Holy Spirit. The Spirit came alongside the disciples, indwelled them, and gave the early church the push they needed to face the challenges ahead.

After Jesus ascended into heaven, the Holy Spirit became the primary agent of the Trinity on earth. He will complete what was begun by the Father and the Son. Though all three expressions of the Godhead are active, the Spirit is taking the lead in this, the final age.

Do you want his power? Direction? Strength? Then "keep in step with the Spirit" (Galatians 5:25 NIV). He directs and leads; you must obey and follow.

PROMISES FROM GOD

If God were to withdraw his Spirit, all life would disappear and mankind would turn again to dust.

—JOB 34:14–15 TLB

"When He, the Spirit of truth, has come, He will guide you into all truth; for He will not speak on His own authority, but whatever He hears He will speak; and He will tell you things to come. He will glorify Me, for He will take of what is Mine and declare it to you. All things that the Father has are Mine. Therefore I said that He will take of Mine and declare it to you."

—JOHN 16:13–15

If we live in the Spirit, let us also walk in the Spirit.

—GALATIANS 5:25

When you heard the true teaching—the Good News about your salvation—you believed in Christ. And in Christ, God put his special mark of ownership on you by giving you the Holy Spirit that he had promised.

—EPHESIANS 1:13 NCV

PRAYING GOD'S PROMISES

Guide me today, Holy Spirit. Show me where you want me to go, whom you want me to talk to, what decision you want me to make. Help me discern your voice over my own and others'. Walk closely with me and whisper truth to me. Forgive me when I listen to my own desires and ignore what you are telling me.

God, I'm so grateful you sent your Spirit to empower me. Thank you for speaking to me and working in me. Stay near to me and help me hear your voice.

Father, you are good—so good that you did not leave us alone on this earth. You left us your Spirit to guide us. Because of your Spirit, I never have to feel alone or afraid. You are with me always. Amen.

I WILL . . .

I will seek to sense, see, and hear the Holy Spirit. I will submit to the Spirit's authority in my life and follow his leading. I will not be afraid of what decision to make and what next step to take—I will trust the Spirit to guide me.

Christ Will Build His Church

"I will build my church, and all the powers of hell will not conquer it."

—MATTHEW 16:18 NLT

UNSHAKABLE HOPE

In Matthew 16, Jesus asked his followers a critical question: "Who do you say that I am?" (Matthew 16:15). Peter, after what might have been a long silence, gave his answer: "You are the Christ, the Son of the living God" (Matthew 16:16).

Every good Hebrew knew the Christ was coming. Someone greater than Abraham, mightier than Moses, a prophet higher than Elijah. The Christ, by definition, means the "ultimate one." He wasn't the final word; he was the only Word.

Jesus, in Peter's confession, was this Christ.

"On this rock, I will build My church," was Jesus' reply (Matthew 16:18). What is the rock he was referring to? What Peter had just confessed—the belief that Jesus was the Messiah.

Everything in Jesus' ministry had led up to this point. The virgin birth. The Nazarene upbringing. Water-walking and cadaver-calling. And now the Carpenter had another project on the table. The same man who formed tables and chairs in Nazareth unveiled a blueprint: "I will build my church."

Rulers will come and go. But the church of Jesus Christ, built on the person of Jesus, will prevail.

If the last two thousand years tell us anything, they tell us the church will succeed. How many nations have come and gone? But the church remains. How many armies have risen and fallen? But the church remains.

In the midst of it all, there is Jesus Christ and his question: "Who do you say that I am?" And there is Jesus Christ and his vow: "I will build my church."

Promises from God

For as the body is one and has many members, but all the members of that one body, being many, are one body, so also is Christ. For by one Spirit we were all baptized into one body—whether Jews or Greeks, whether slaves or free—and have all been made to drink into one Spirit. For in fact the body is not one member but many.

—1 Corinthians 12:12–14

Speaking the truth in love, may grow up in all things into Him who is the head—Christ—from whom the whole body, joined and knit together by what every joint supplies, according to the effective working by which every part does its share, causes growth of the body for the edifying of itself in love.

—Ephesians 4:15–16

All things were created through Him and for Him. And He is before all things, and in Him all things consist. And He is the head of the body, the church, who is the beginning, the firstborn from the dead, that in all things He may have the preeminence.

—Colossians 1:16–18

PRAYING GOD'S PROMISES

Jesus, you are the head of the church. You reign supreme at the right hand of the Father. What you have set out to accomplish in your church and in my heart, you will accomplish. You are the Messiah, the one who is worthy of my praise.

Lord, may your will be done in me. Root out every selfish and prideful desire. Work in me and through me. May the work that I do be the work of building your church, stone by stone. May I desire to be a part of your body, serving your church for your glory rather than seeking after my own desires.

Thank you, Lord, for the physical church as well as the spiritual church. Thank you for my fellow believers. Strengthen us. Strengthen your church. May we build our communities and our lives on your promises. Amen.

I WILL . . .

I will align my life with God's forever family, the church. I will trust that Jesus is the Messiah. What he builds will never fall. He reigns over this earth, and he reigns over me. Nations and armies will rise and fall, but God's church will remain forever.

God Will Meet Your Needs

God shall supply all your
need according to His riches
in glory by Christ Jesus.
—PHILIPPIANS 4:19

UNSHAKABLE HOPE

If you had the choice, if you were offered a palace with no Christ or a prison with Christ, which would you choose?

In ancient Rome, the emperor Nero had the palace, but no Christ. The legacy of his reign is deceit, fear, murder, and a severe abuse of power. Eventually, he died alone. Deified, but alone. Rich, but alone. Powerful, but alone. In the end, he had everything except happiness.

Paul, on the other hand, had nothing but happiness. Yet he literally had nothing. He was impoverished. He had no health. He was imprisoned during Nero's time. His tired body carried the marks of whippings, shipwrecks, and disease.

But if Paul were given half a chance, he would tell you the story of stories. He would tilt his large head to the side and smile a wry smile. He would speak of the light that left him blind and the voice that left him speechless.

"Saul, Saul," Jesus spoke (Acts 9:4).

If you were to ask Paul to choose between the palace and the prison, he would be quick to answer. *My purse may be empty, but my Father's is not.* "My God will meet all your needs according to the riches of his glory in Christ Jesus" (Philippians 4:19 NIV).

That's the promise. That was the discovery of Paul. That is the hope of the believer. God is in charge of your life. Though your "Nero" might attempt to incarcerate you, your Lord will provide for you. He will give you everything you need. A palace with no Christ is a prison. A prison with Christ is a palace.

PROMISES FROM GOD

The young lions lack and suffer hunger; but those who seek the LORD shall not lack any good thing.

—PSALM 34:10

Happy is he who has the God of Jacob for his help, whose hope is in the LORD his God, who made heaven and earth, the sea, and all that *is* in them; who keeps truth forever, who executes justice for the oppressed, who gives food to the hungry. The LORD gives freedom to the prisoners.

—PSALM 146:5–7

"For your Father knows the things you have need of before you ask Him."

—MATTHEW 6:8

"Are not two sparrows sold for a copper coin? And not one of them falls to the ground apart from your Father's will. But the very hairs of your head are all numbered. Do not fear therefore; you are of more value than many sparrows."

—MATTHEW 10:29–31

PRAYING GOD'S PROMISES

Lord, you are the provider and giver of all. Nothing about me is hidden from you. You can count every hair on my head. You know all of my needs before I can even ask for them.

Sometimes it's tempting for me to believe I can rely on myself for what I need. Instead of trusting you to provide, I think I can look out for myself. I fear not having enough. And when I do have enough, it never feels like it.

But you have promised to meet my needs out of your glorious riches. Remind me of your kind and generous provision. Thank you for taking care of me and meeting all of my needs.

Allow me to find full satisfaction in you, Father. I know you have provided for me and you have been faithful to me in the past. Continue to do so. Build up my trust in you. Your ultimate provision came in the form of your Son, Jesus. May that truth feel real to me today. Amen.

I WILL . . .

I will trust God to meet my needs. I will
not try to provide for myself. I will not
fall into the trap of always wanting more.
In God I will find my full satisfaction.
I will believe in the promise that he
cares for me and will take care of me.

Justice Will Prevail

*He has appointed a day on
which He will judge the world.*
—ACTS 17:31

UNSHAKABLE HOPE

t's not fair. When did you learn those words? What deed exposed you to the imbalanced scales of life? Did a car wreck leave you fatherless? Did friends forget you, a teacher ignore you, an adult abuse you?

How long will injustice flourish? God's answer is direct: not long. Scripture reveals a somber promise: "He has appointed a day on which He will judge the world" (Acts 17:31).

"Judgment Day" is an unpopular term. We disdain judgment, but we value justice, yet the second is impossible without the first. One can't have justice without judgment. For that reason "we must all appear before the judgment seat of Christ, that each one may receive the things done in the body, according to what he has done, whether good or bad" (2 Corinthian 5:10).

From his throne Jesus will forever balance the scales of fairness. He will do so through three declarations:

- He will publicly pardon his people (Romans 3:23–26).
- He will applaud the service of his servants (1 Corinthians 4:5).
- He will honor the wishes of the wicked (Romans 1:21, 23).

Justice will prevail.

Remember, God understands injustice. He will right all wrongs and heal all wounds. He has prepared a place where life will be finally and forever . . . just.

Promises from God

Lord, how long will You look on? Rescue me from their destructions, my precious life from the lions. I will give You thanks in the great assembly; I will praise You among many people.

—Psalm 35:17–18

Why do you pass judgment on your brother? Or you, why do you despise your brother? For we will all stand before the judgment seat of God; for it is written, "As I live, says the Lord, every knee shall bow to me, and every tongue shall confess to God." So then each of us will give an account of himself to God.

—Romans 14:10–12 esv

He will bring to light what is hidden in darkness and will expose the motives of the heart. At that time each will receive their praise from God.

—1 Corinthians 4:5 niv

For God is not unjust to forget your work and labor of love which you have shown toward His name, in that you have ministered to the saints, and do minister.

—Hebrews 6:10

PRAYING GOD'S PROMISES

Heavenly Father, forgive me for doubting your goodness and your justice. When things don't go my way or when events happen that are beyond my understanding, I may wonder, How long will you look on?

Forgive me also when I pass judgment on others. Only you know their hearts. Give me grace to get to know and understand people truly rather than judging them.

I know you have offered the greatest promise in Jesus. In him, I am saved from my own sin, and I can trust that justice will be done. It's not up to me to ensure that everything in life is fair. It is up to me to serve you as best I can. Help me surrender the rest to you.

God, you are the great Judge. You know all of our sin. You know the motivations we have in our hearts. Through your love and grace, you seek justice fiercely.

Thank you for your good judgment. In your mercy, you sent Jesus, whose righteousness has saved me. I am forever grateful for this promise. Amen.

I WILL . . .

I will respect God's justice and delight
in God's grace. I will not consider
myself the judge of fairness. I will
trust God to that job. He is the great
Judge. I will look forward to the day
when all is made right by him.

God Makes All Things New

Then He who sat on the throne
said, "Behold, I make all things
new." And He said to me, "Write, for
these words are true and faithful."
—REVELATION 21:5

UNSHAKABLE HOPE

Life on earth meets the basic definition of an airport: a place to wait until your flight home is called.

You were never meant to stay on this form of earth. You were made for more than life in a terminal. And you can thank John for this glimpse of your true destination: "Then I, John, saw the holy city, New Jerusalem, coming down out of heaven from God, prepared as a bride adorned for her husband" (Revelation 21:2).

John's description of the New Jerusalem stretches the imagination: fourteen hundred miles in length, width, and height. Large enough to contain the land mass from the Appalachians to the West Coast. The city stands as tall as it does wide. The New Jerusalem would have six hundred thousand floors, ample space for billions of people. Ample space for you.

This life hasn't always had space for you, has it? When did you discover the congestion of this world? The school had no space for you. Your father's schedule had no space for you. You learned early the finite amount of resources. Only so much time, only so many seats.

But God promises a spacious city. Every page and promise of the Bible invites and excites us with the lure of a new day, a new earth, and a new kingdom, where he will "make all things new" (Revelation 21:5). Because of this, we do not give up. Instead, we lift up our eyes and look. The new city is coming.

PROMISES FROM GOD

The created world itself can hardly wait for what's coming next.

—ROMANS 8:19 THE MESSAGE

So we do not give up. Our physical body is becoming older and weaker, but our spirit inside us is made new every day. We have small troubles for a while now, but they are helping us gain an eternal glory that is much greater than the troubles. We set our eyes not on what we see but on what we cannot see. What we see will last only a short time, but what we cannot see will last forever.

—2 CORINTHIANS 4:16–18 NCV

In keeping with his promise we are looking forward to a new heaven and a new earth, where righteousness dwells.

—2 PETER 3:13 NIV

No longer will there be any curse. The throne of God and of the Lamb will be in the city, and his servants will serve him.

—REVELATION 22:3 NIV

PRAYING GOD'S PROMISES

God, you are the Creator of this earth as well as the one to come. You reign in the here and now, and you will reign for eternity. This kingdom is yours; it has always been yours, and it always will be.

One day the pains of this world will be long gone, and I will get to see you face to face. Until then, continue making me new. Refine me. Help me to keep eternity in mind, making the most of my days and showing others your renewing love.

Thank you for making all things new. Because I am a part of your family, I will always belong. I am so grateful to be covered by your grace and mercy. Amen.

I WILL . . .

I will fix my eyes on things above.
Because I know that this world is
not my home, I will keep eternity
in sight. I will find belonging in
God's family. And I will live as an
inheritor of the New Jerusalem, where
God will make all things new.

Hope Is an Anchor for Your Soul

We have this hope as an anchor for the soul, firm and secure. It enters the inner sanctuary behind the curtain, where our forerunner, Jesus, has entered on our behalf.

—HEBREWS 6:19–20 NIV

UNSHAKABLE HOPE

Everyone is anchored to something. A retirement account or a résumé. Some are tethered to a person or career position. Yet these are surface objects. Would you anchor your boat to another boat? You want something that goes deeper and holds firmer than other floating vessels. But when you anchor to the things of this world, are you not doing the same? Can a retirement account survive a depression? Can good health weather a disease? There is no guarantee.

Ask yourself, *Is what I'm hooked to stronger than what I'll go through?*

Salty sailors would urge you to hook on to something hidden and solid. Don't trust the buoy on the water, don't trust the sailors in the other boat, and don't trust the other boat. When the storm hits, trust no one but God.

Hebrews says, "We have this hope as an anchor for the soul, firm and secure. It enters the inner sanctuary behind the curtain, where our forerunner, Jesus, has entered on our behalf" (Hebrews 6:19–20 NIV). Our anchor, in other words, is set in the very throne room of God, and the rope is strong. It will never break free. Why? Because it is beyond the reach of the devil and under the care of Christ. Since no one can take your Christ, no one can take your hope.

Secure your anchor in God. Build your life on his promises. Since his promises are unbreakable, your hope will be unshakable. The winds will still blow. The rain will still fall. But in the end, you will be standing on the promises of God.

PROMISES FROM GOD

His pleasure is not in the strength of the horse, nor his delight in the legs of the warrior; the LORD delights in those who fear him, who put their hope in his unfailing love.

—PSALM 147:10–11 NIV

But those who wait on the LORD shall renew their strength; they shall mount up with wings like eagles, they shall run and not be weary, they shall walk and not faint.

—ISAIAH 40:31

Having promise of the life that now is and of that which is to come. This is a faithful saying and worthy of all acceptance. For to this end we both labor and suffer reproach, because we trust in the living God, who is the Savior of all men, especially of those who believe.

—1 TIMOTHY 4:8–10

Now may the God of hope fill you with all joy and peace in believing, that you may abound in hope by the power of the Holy Spirit.

—ROMANS 15:13

PRAYING GOD'S PROMISES

Dear God, you are my unshakable hope. Your promises are unbreakable. You never waver. You are faithful to the end. My hope cannot be anchored to anything less than your promises.

You know my heart, and you know that I have idols. Wealth, other people, status, achievement, my health—I anchor my hope to these far too many times. Each time I do, I am disappointed. They are like buoys floating on the surface compared to your promises.

Forgive me for those times when I don't put my hope in you. May I rest in your promises once again. May any fear, anxiety, or confusion I feel subside in light of you as my anchor. Allow me to let go of needing answers and a solution and, instead, hold on to your unfailing promises. Help me let go of these false idols and turn my eyes to the true anchor I have in you.

Thank you for being my great anchor. Thank you for the unshakable hope I have in your unbreakable promises. Amen.

I WILL . . .

I will anchor my soul to the hope of
Christ. I will not put my trust in earthly
things. I will know and believe that when
I am anchored in Christ nothing can
take my hope away. It is deeply rooted
in him. Because of God's unbreakable
promises, I have unshakable hope.

Notes

1. Dr. Herbert Lockyer, *All the Promises of the Bible* (Grand Rapids: Zondervan, 1962), 10.
2. Louis J. Cameli, *The Devil You Don't Know: Recognizing and Resisting Evil in Everyday Life* (Notre Dame, IN: Ave Maria Press, 2011), 79.
3. Mark Mayberry, "The City of Babylon," *Truth Magazine,* February 17, 2000, http://truthmagazine.com/archives/volume44/V44021708.htm.